SAiNT PeTeR

CTS Children's Books

Contents

Text by Elena Pascoletti

Illustrations by Tommaso D'Incalci

Translated by Simone Finaldi

Saint Peter: Published 2013 by The Incorporated Catholic Truth Society, 40-46 Harleyford Road, London SE11 5AY. Tel: 020 7640 0042; Fax: 020 7640 0046; www.CTSbooks.org Copyright © 2013 The Incorporated Catholic Truth Society in this English-language edition.

ISBN: 978 1 86082 888 1   CTS Code CH 49

Translated from the original Italian Edition **San Pietro** - ISBN 978-88-6124-433-7, published by Il Pozzo di Giacobbe, Gruppo Editoriale S.R.L., Cortile San Teodoro, 3, 91100 Trapani (TP), Italy © 2013 Il Pozzo di Giacobbe.

A FISHERMAN FROM GALILEE

In the north of Palestine, the land of Jesus, there was a large lake called Gennesaret, which is also called the Sea of Tiberius or the Sea of Galilee. Around the shore of the lake there were many fishing villages; one of them was called Bethesda: where Simon, son of John was born. Simon and his brother Andrew had become very good fishermen. Every day before dawn, they went out onto the lake in their boat together with two friends, James and John, their father Zebedee and some helpers. At the end of each day if the catch was good, after putting away the boat, they would empty all the baskets and laugh happily after all their hard work. When there were not many fish, they would sit and clean the nets in silence, hoping that tomorrow they would catch many more.

SIMON'S BOAT

That was exactly what happened one day; they worked for many hours and had not caught a thing! Tired out, they went back to Capernaum, where Simon lived after he had married, and started cleaning the nets.

Something was happening, and every now and then, Simon looked up from his work. He could see that everyone was staring at a man and trying to get closer to him to hear his words. The man was Jesus of Nazareth. Simon looked up again and saw that Jesus was coming towards him.

"I need your boat!" Jesus told him. Simon was very surprised, but let him get into the boat. Jesus spoke to him again, "Let's move away from the shore, so everyone can hear."

Sitting in the boat and looking at all the people in front of him, Jesus spoke to them about the love of God for everyone.

Then he said to Simon, "Throw your nets into the deep water for a catch!" Simon answered quickly, "What do you mean? We worked all night and did not even catch one fish…" While he spoke, Simon felt in his heart that he should trust this man.

After a moment he added, "Because you told me, I will go fishing again."

The fishermen all got back into the boat with Jesus and something incredible happened: the nets became so full of fish that the boat was nearly sinking! Everyone was amazed that Jesus's words were so powerful and could do such amazing things. Simon felt confused and very small and unimportant, but Jesus comforted him, then told him, "Follow me! From now on, you will be a Fisher of men." Simon bravely left the boats, the nets, everything and followed him. It was the start of a great adventure.

A NEW NAME

Simon was a simple, generous and kind man. He did not know where Jesus would take him, or what it meant to be a "Fisher of men", but he felt that his words were not like those of other teachers, they were words that were alive and spoke strongly to his heart. Travelling along the roads of Galilee, Jesus announced that God was near to everybody, especially those who were poor, humble and small.

Many people followed him but some were specially chosen by Jesus, and, like Simon, they left everything so that they could be always with him. They were Andrew, Simon's brother and James, John and Philip their friend from Bethesda. Then there were: Bartholomew, Matthew, Thomas, another James the son of Alfius, Jude, Simon the Canaanite and Judas Iscariot. Altogether they were twelve.

Jesus had great plans for Simon who he kept close to him. He did something to Simon that he did not do to any of the others of the twelve: he changed his name! Jesus said to him, "You are Simon, son of John but from now on you will be called Cephas."

In Jesus's language, Cephas meant rock. It was much more than a nickname, it was more like a very important task. Simon had to be as strong as a rock, his faith in Jesus had to be solid and stable like a well cut stone on which a building is founded. The name was so important that it was translated into Greek as Petros, who we call Peter! That was his mission, to become a rock, but before that, he would go through difficult times; he would learn about doubt, fear and weakness.

TRAVELLING

Jesus was always travelling! He went up and down his country teaching people to trust God and speak to him like to a loving father who already knows what we need. He said, "Ask and you shall receive. Seek and you will find!"

When he went to Capernaum, Jesus and his friends stayed in Peter's house. One day, they found Peter's mother-in-law in bed, very ill. Jesus came near and looked at her and she got up, feeling better and happy to serve him.

Jesus was full of love for those who suffered and he would free them from their illnesses. Often the people who came to him were very sick or nearly dying. Jesus was glad when people came to him, trusting in him and believing he could heal them.

One day, one of the leaders of the synagogue, called Jairus, came forward out of the crowd. He had come to ask Jesus to come and visit his house, his little 12-year-old girl was dying. Everyone thought it was too late to help her, everyone except Jairus! It was important for Peter to see what having faith in Jesus could mean, so Jesus went with Peter, James and John to Jairus's house. Sending everyone else further off, he took the dead girl by the hand and gave her back to her parents alive and well!

It was now time for Jesus's twelve friends to become apostles, so he sent them out to the villages of Galilee, two by two, to bring the people news of great joy: that the Kingdom of God was very near to them and they had to live in a new

way and only do good! Jesus gave them the power to heal people and to raise the dead through his name. The apostles returned from their mission filled with joy and enthusiasm, telling of all the amazing things that had happened.

THE WORDS OF JESUS

The words of Jesus were not always easy to put into practice: for example he said, "Love your enemies!" Peter wanted to understand these words and so one day, he asked the Master, "If my brother hurts me, how many times must I forgive him? Up to seven times?" Maybe he thought that was many times but Jesus surprised him by saying, "I won't say up to seven times but seventy times seven!" That means we must always forgive, just as God forgives us. Jesus touched everyone with his words; using parables, he explained how much God loves us and what he wants us to do. Sometimes, people stayed listening to him all day long.

One evening, his friends told him that all the people listening were hungry; it was too late for them to go into the villages nearby to get food.

With them, there was a boy with five loaves and two fish. How would that help so many people? Jesus took the loaves and fish, blessed them and broke them, giving them to his disciples to hand out to the people and the food did not run out!

Nobody could believe it. Jesus had fed more than five thousand people! After this great miracle, people wanted to make him king but it was not what Jesus wanted!

He explained that he had come to give people another kind of food: his own body to eat! At those words, many of his disciples were sad and abandoned him. Jesus asked the twelve if they too wished to leave him. Peter found the words of Jesus difficult to understand as well but he answered for them all, "Lord, to whom shall we go? You alone have words of life!"

THE FAITH OF PETER

Jesus said goodbye to the people and then went away alone to pray, while Peter and the others waited for him in a boat.

Later it was dark and the sea was choppy. Among the waves, they could see someone coming towards them, walking on the water! Some of them screamed thinking it was a ghost and they were all frightened. But a voice reassured them, "Courage, it is I, do not be afraid." "Can it really be Jesus?" Peter asked himself. He wanted to be sure, so he asked, "Lord, if it is you, tell me to come to you over the waters." He heard the answer, "Come!" So he bravely got out of the boat and he began walking towards Jesus, over the water. Then he became afraid and began to sink.

Jesus seized his hand and said to him, "Why did you doubt, man of little faith?" Jesus was stronger than the wind and the waves, the lake or the storm. Each day, he amazed them with what he said and did. Each day there were new things to understand and to learn! Who was Jesus? It was very important for the apostles to know the answer to this question. One day he asked them that exact question himself, "Who do you say I am?" Peter stepped forward and answered on behalf of them all, "You are the Christ, the son of the living God!" meaning the messiah, the saviour his people were

waiting for. Jesus saw that Peter, helped by God, had told the truth and said, "You are Peter and on this rock I will build my Church, I will give you the keys to the kingdom of heaven."

Peter's faith was a great gift for the whole Church. Jesus gave him the task of guiding and helping her through every difficulty, and leading her into the glory of his kingdom.

TO JERUSALEM!

From that moment, Jesus began to tell his friends what was going to happen to him. Jesus was getting ready to go to Jerusalem; there he would suffer and die and then rise again. This is what it meant "to be the messiah"; this was the plan of love and salvation that God had prepared. At these words, Peter became angry: something so horrible should never happen, he thought. He spoke to the Master alone and told him off! Jesus was very clear with Peter, "You think like men, not like God!" Jesus told Peter to get behind him, to be humble, to be obedient and to follow him. Even when the journey is hard, it is Jesus who shows us the way.

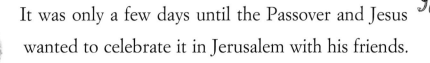

It was only a few days until the Passover and Jesus wanted to celebrate it in Jerusalem with his friends.

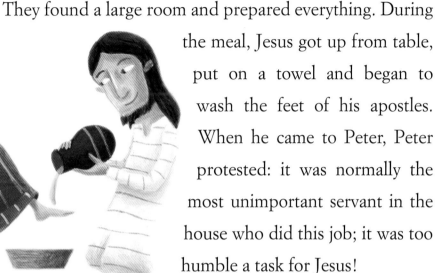

They found a large room and prepared everything. During the meal, Jesus got up from table, put on a towel and began to wash the feet of his apostles. When he came to Peter, Peter protested: it was normally the most unimportant servant in the house who did this job; it was too humble a task for Jesus!

So Jesus explained to Peter, "Now, you do not understand what I have done but later, you will understand." After Jesus had finished, he said, "If I, the Lord and Master, have washed your feet, you too should wash each other's feet."

It was another lesson for them not to forget: it was not a competition to be the first or the most important, but they must serve others with love, as Jesus did in that moment.

THE DARKEST NIGHT

That night was the longest and most difficult night of Peter's life. Jesus had told them something terrible: it was one of them who was going to betray him! Everybody was very worried. Jesus got up from table and went out to pray; he went to a garden at the foot of the Mount of Olives. Peter loved Jesus his Master and said he would never abandon him. But Jesus, who knew Peter's heart, sadly told him, "This night, before the cock crows, you will deny me three times."

Then Jesus left the disciples, taking with him his dearest friends, Peter, James and John. "Stay and pray with me" he said. Full of pain, he prayed intensely to his father, to have the strength to offer his life.

16

But his friends were not able to wait and pray with Jesus.

They woke up when they heard people coming; it was Judas with the temple guards who had come to arrest Jesus. Peter wanted to defend him; he quickly drew his sword and wounded the high priest's servant. Jesus told Peter off and healed the wound. Then everyone ran away. Peter was very afraid but still followed him from far away, While they were asking Jesus questions, Peter was in the courtyard of the High Priest's palace, warming his hands by the fire. A young servant girl recognised him, she was sure she had seen him before, he was one of those people who was always with Jesus! Three times, Peter denied it with all his strength!

Then he heard a cock crow. He remembered what the Master had said and understood that he was very weak. He burst into tears and wept, asking for forgiveness because he had not been faithful to Jesus.

PETER, FISHERMAN AND SHEPHERD

Jesus had died on the cross three days before. Peter and his companions stayed locked in a room, they were too frightened to go out into the street. The women who were with them decided to go and visit the tomb where the body of the Lord Jesus lay. It was still early when the apostles heard another knock on the door; the women, full of joy, told them that Jesus had risen! So Peter and John ran to the tomb and saw that what the women had told them was true. They were still fearful but Jesus himself came to them and they too were full of joy and wonder: the Lord was truly risen!

Jesus appeared to them many times after that day. One night, Peter went fishing with some of the other apostles but did not catch anything. At dawn, they saw a man on the shore who told them to throw out their nets again. So, just like on the day Jesus had called him, Peter's nets were filled with fish and he jumped into the water to swim to his Master!

Jesus ate some fish with them and then he wanted to speak to Peter alone. Jesus asked if Peter really loved him, more than the rest. Peter, who had been through difficult and testing moments, answered that yes, with all his weaknesses and limitations, he loved him.

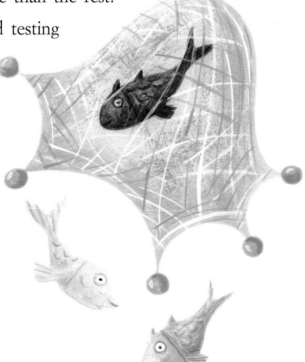

Jesus now entrusted the Church, all the sheep and lambs he loved so much and had given his life for, to Peter saying, "Look after my sheep!" Now Peter understood what Jesus had said after the first miraculous catch of fish, now he would be a "Fisher of men"!

The apostles were united and always prayed together. Jesus had told them they would spread the good news across the whole world but they had to wait, they would not be able to do it on their own.

During the feast of Pentecost, Peter and the others received the gift Jesus had promised, the Holy Spirit, which made them strong and brave. They went out onto the streets of Jerusalem, full of joy.

They spoke about the Master to everyone they met, Jews and foreigners, and each person heard it in their own language! They were amazed, so Peter spoke and explained that it was a gift of the Holy Spirit. He announced that Jesus was God's son and that he had really risen from the dead; many people asked Peter to be baptised and became Christians.

The apostles witnessed openly to their faith and performed miracles in the name of Jesus. The Jewish priests wanted to stop them, so they put Peter and John in prison.

20

They did let them go but told them not to speak about Jesus anymore. Peter said that was impossible, "We cannot keep quiet about what we saw and heard!"

Some time later, the king, Herod Agrippa put him in prison again, but he was happy, trusting in God's help. All the community prayed strongly that Peter would soon be free and God granted their prayer.

An angel came to him at night, unlocked his chains and led him out of the prison.

Peter thought it was a vision but when he understood that the angel had really set him free, he went to the disciple Mark's house, were many people were praying. When they saw him, they cried out in happiness.

LEADER OF THE CHURCH

Peter guided the Church for many years, in Jerusalem, in Antioch and in Rome, where he announced the gospel and was the head of the Christian community for twenty-five years.

In the New Testament there are two letters of Saint Peter. As shepherd of the whole Church, Peter encouraged the Christians to stay faithful to the Lord Jesus, even in the most difficult times.

He himself showed his faith, now as strong as a rock, by dying as a martyr in Rome when the emperor Nero persecuted the Christians. It is said he was nailed to the cross upside down because he did not feel worthy to be crucified in the same way as his lord. This was probably in the year 67 AD. The Church venerates him very much, together with Saint Paul, on their feast day, the 29th June.

AN IMAGE OF
SAINT PETER

A PRAYER

Thank you, O Lord, for loving us

and choosing us as we are.

Please, Jesus, help me discover the adventure

you have prepared for my life.

Whatever my path will be,

I ask that I may be always simple and generous, like Peter,

to follow you and leave behind things that do not matter.

Make me curious, like Peter, who asked you many questions

because he understood that your words are truth.

May I be humble like Peter and admit my mistakes

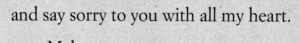

and say sorry to you with all my heart.

Make me a true, courageous

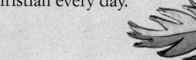

and joyful Christian every day.